To Dad,
wishing you a very happy birthday - late of course.
All love Pam xxx

AUSTRALIAN ABORIGINES

Shadows in a Landscape

Photography: Laurence Le Guay
Text: Suzanne Falkiner

First published by James H Coleman
Globe Publishing Company Sydney.

Set in Plantin Medium type by
Hartland and Hyde, Sydney.

Production: David Heweston Sydney.

Wholly set up, printed and bound by
Dai Nippon, Hong Kong.

Concept and design Laurence Le Guay.

Photographed with Hasselblad, Nikon and Rolleiflex
cameras on Kodak Ektachrome film.

National Library of Australia card:
ISBN 0 9597359 2 5.

First edition 1980.

Contents

For Tony and Judy Chisholm
"ANNINGIE", Northern Territory

List of Plates

Preface

Australians are city-dwellers, they inhabit the sprawling cities of the coasts, leaving the vast, dry inland of the continent to a small minority of the population. They look inward to the intricate machinery of city life, allowing only a small input of information from the outside. The cultures with which they identify are the cultures which hold their roots: those of England, Europe, the Western world. From this spectrum the Australian Aborigines are excluded, and thus remain largely unknown.

A race of mysterious origin, falling outside the three great groups of human types, unlike any other except for physical similarities with some obscure tribes of Sri Lanka and southern India, the Australian Aborigines are not susceptible to easy explanations. And they make little effort to be understood. Their culture is a fragile web of oral traditions and complex myths stored in the collective mind of a tribal people, unsupported by written words or technological recording devices. It is a culture which disintegrates readily when the invasion of a more materialistic society breaks down the tenuous link between generations. And having existed in almost complete isolation for so long, the Aborigines have developed no mechanisms to prevent this from happening.

Much has been written and said by, for and about Aboriginal Australians in the last few years, from a number of different arenas. Various groups of people sympathetic to the Aborigines have made a great effort to disseminate information about them, yet the audience they are reaching is limited. At the performances of Aboriginal dance, at the exhibitions of modern and traditional art, at the films, at the political meetings, it is always the same faces which appear. At the same time, touring Aboriginal dance groups are meeting with more interest and appreciation in Europe and America than on their home ground, and irreplaceable examples of pre-European and contemporary Aboriginal art are fast disappearing into private collections in the United States. It would almost seem that Australian Aborigines are experiencing the same fate that other Australian dancers and artists experienced a decade ago: that of being faced with the necessity of 'making it overseas' before being accepted in their own country. The Aboriginal presence is becoming stronger in Australia, yet the mass of Australian society remains untouched.

This book is not an anthropological, sociological or political study. Rather it is intended as a series of impressions of a race of people and the forces acting for and against them, an image of the Australian Aboriginal in a country in which he is largely displaced. It is an attempt to further the understanding of European Australians of the race they are reading about daily in the newspapers, but have rarely actually met. It is also a tribute to a joyous and gentle people who, mainly through lack of understanding, have long been forced into the position of fringe-dwellers and ghosts.

During the last great Ice Age there were times when, due to vast accretions of ice in the northern hemisphere, sea levels were sixty to ninety metres lower than they are at present. Java, Sumatra and Borneo were part of the Asian mainland, and this was separated from the Australian continent, as it was then, by stretches of water of less than a hundred and sixty kilometres. Over this archipelago a people in some form of boats were thus able to make their way to the great southern continent. Here, as the great ice sheets melted and isolated the land-mass that is Australia today, the Aborigines existed unmolested for forty thousand years.

There are many sacred places for Aborigines, places of their Dreaming, where the spirits of the dead and the living cross over and intermingle. For every tribal Aboriginal, the world is both the physical environment and a closely interrelated sphere of supernatural forces which are vastly important to his survival. The Dreaming, or Dreamtime, is a state from which his spirit originated and to which it will eventually return, and also an actual period of history during which the world was created and the place of all creatures within it ordained. The cycle of the seasons, the fertility of land and animals, the continuation of life, are all subject to the spirit world with its hierarchy of ancestral beings, malevolent spirits and creative forces. Thus history and myth combine in an ambiguous area. Dance, chant, ceremony, painting and carving re-create past or legendary events, ensuring general well-being through communication with the spirits. Similarly every tribal Aboriginal has his 'country', a physical region with which his spirit is linked. If the sacred places within these regions are defiled, the ceremonies and laws associated with them lost, then the meaning of life is lost.

Ayers Rock – Uluru –
Dreaming place of the Pitjantjatjara tribe

Devils Marbles, Northern Territory

Katherine Gorge, Northern Territory

Full blood Aboriginal girl Unmugera tribe, Northern Territory

Pride, in a white race, often appea
to be an indestructible thing.
In a black man it would seem to b
rather more fragile.
It is a rare thing to see pride
in the face of an Aboriginal today.

Full blood Aboriginal man, Walbiri Tribe, Northern Territory 25

Aboriginal boy, Northern Territory

Aboriginal child with dead bird

Bustard or Wild Turkey

Emu

Birds, mammals, plants, insects, reptiles, sun, moon, stars, fire, water
all assume individual dreamtime totemic and ancestral significance
for Aborigines.

Kangaroo

Grass trees or blackboys

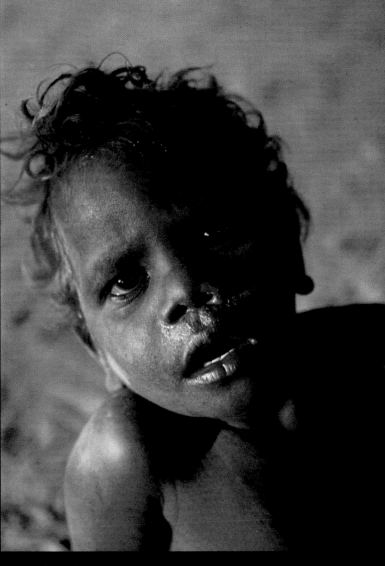

Head of a child, Arnhem Land

Young mother with child Northern Territory

Full blood male Aborigine

Children with Tribal markings

Corroboree Group

Mother & children

Shirley Smith, known as Mum Shirl, was about 15 or 16 when she first visited a prisoner in Sydney's Long Bay Jail. That prisoner was her seventeen-year-old brother. But Shirley Smith kept on visiting the jail long after her brother was released. Because, she will tell you, there were too many lonely people still inside.

Later, making her headquarters in the parish hall at St Vincent's Church at Redfern, Sydney, Shirley Smith started taking care of neglected children, unwed mothers, lonely migrants, alcoholics, juvenile offenders and adult prisoners turned over to her by the courts.

Now, 36 years on, Shirley Smith, MBE, has a government pass into jails all over NSW. She is mainly responsible for the starting of the Aboriginal Medical Service and the Aboriginal Legal Service in Sydney in the early 1970s. She also has the love of an estimated 5,811 children who have passed through her hands and who will probably continue to call her Mum Shirl all their lives.

Shirley Smith was born into a mixed Aboriginal and Irish family on the Erambie mission at West Cowra sometime around 1921. She cannot read or write. She did not receive a formal education because she was born an epileptic, and was not allowed to go to school in case this mysterious affliction was contagious. Since then she believes she has learnt a lesson of love from this disease: she has memories of coming to herself on crowded streets to find she was being stepped around by passers-by who believed she was drunk. Her childhood, spent in a tin shack with a dirt floor, was largely influenced by her grandfather, a fullblood member of the Wiradjury tribe who taught her tribal ways. Of him she says, 'He was a man gifted with the ways of the spirits, he taught me love, he breathed his spirit into me, and when he died he left me his peace.' She was also brought up a member of the Roman Catholic Church by her mother, but it is to a black saint, St Martin de Pourres, to whom she prays especially. When Mother Teresa of Calcutta visited Australia in 1975 it was Shirley Smith, then unknown to many white Australians, that she wanted to meet.

Shirley Smith is an articulate woman. She believes she exists to pass on the Aboriginal spirit from her forefathers' generation to future ones. In an unaccustomed moment of rest she muses, 'Corruption starts to exist where waters don't run free. It's the same with people, with people who aren't free. That's why you'll find that running water, free-flowing rivers and creeks, are important to Aborigines . . .'

But Shirley Smith is also a sad, spirited, angry, loving woman. There isn't much she hasn't seen. When she was made a Parent of the Year in 1979 she accepted the award saying, 'I don't want this, but I'm taking it on behalf of all the children I've buried.' The four television stations present at the ceremony chose to cut this particular comment from their coverage of the event, and, speaking about it afterwards, Shirley Smith was crying.

Earth mounds built by thousands of grass eating termites which
sometimes reach a height of 6 metres with a diameter of 2 metres,
and a long axis invariably running true-north-south. These voracious
insects in their winged stage provide the aborigines with a
ready source of food. At the time of their spectacular swarming
they are dug out and placed on hot stones in a coolamon
receptacle and as their wings are singed off they congeal
in a thick buttery substance.

Although the returning boomerang is an image inextricably associated with
Aborigines in the minds of Europeans, it was not used throughout Australia.
Following aerodynamic principles, the lower surface of the returning
boomerang is flat and the upper convex. The two ends are sometimes
twisted in opposing directions; so that when thrown it rotates on its own axis,
describes a wide arc and returns to the thrower. Sometimes it was used
to kill birds or frighten quarry towards a hunter or into a trap.
In comparison, the hunting or fighting boomerang is heavier
and less symmetrically shaped.

Full blood girl with dingo pup

Aborigines camped in dry watercourse

Seeds in the desert

Drought I

Witchetty grubs infest the roots of certain small trees and are dug for by women and older children who can tell at a glance which trees will be productive.
Aborigines often eat them raw as well as cooked and regard the insect as a great delicacy.

Aboriginal camp in dry river bed

Aboriginal group, Northern Territory

To make a bark painting, the artist splits off a cylindrical piece of bark from the trunk of a tree and dries and straightens it into a flat surface over a fire. The inner surface is scraped and the edges trimmed, and a vegetable derivative is applied as a fixative. The major outlines of the design are sketched in with a fibrous twig 'brush', the more detailed work such as cross-hatching may be done with a brush made of human hair. Traditional colours are those available, the colours of the earth, red, white, yellow and black, which are ground in a stone mortar and mixed with water. Ochres from different regions are highly prized and may be traded from group to group. Subject matter may include totemic animals and plants, ancestral beings, environmental elements such as clouds, rain, waves and landforms, or abstract designs. Different styles and subject matter are peculiar to different regions, perhaps the best known to Europeans are the 'X-ray' figures of Western Arnhem Land and the 'Mimi' art of the same region.

Artist: Peter Maralwonga
(courtesy Hogarth Gallery)

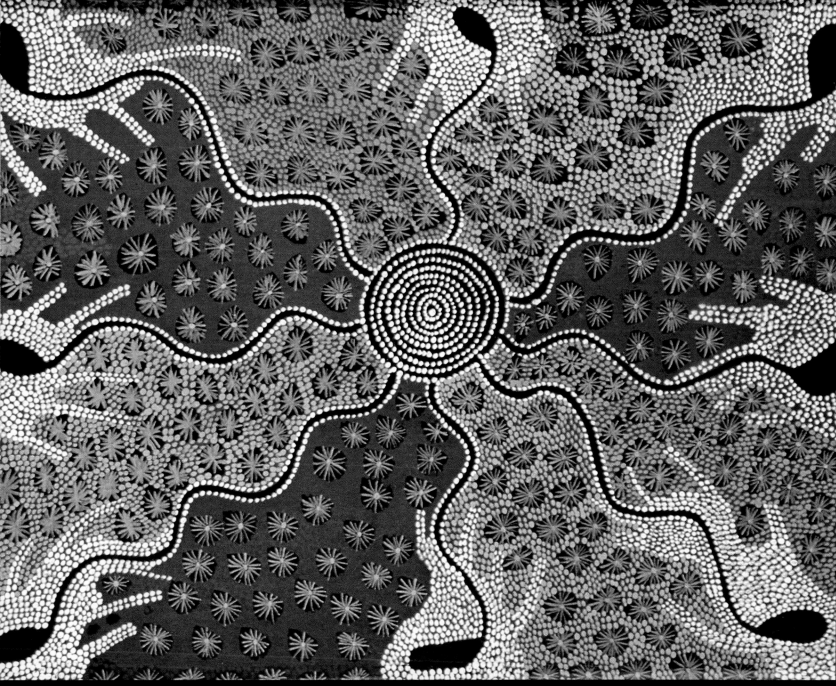

Elaborate ground mosaics once created and used for
traditional ceremonial purposes are now prepared on
board, canvas or galvanised iron using contemporary
paints and brushes at Papunya Aboriginal settlement,
250 km west of Alice Springs.
Artist: Billy Stockman

Aboriginal stockman
& white child
Cattle Station,
Northern Territory

Aboriginal women gathering firewood,
Northern Territory

Territory cattle station

Territory Aboriginal settlement

Women dressed for Corroboree

Women & children dancing
Northern Territory

Children playing at a waterhole

Tribal Warriors circa 1910
Courtesy Australian Museum.

Settlement living, Northern Territory

Settlement family, Northern Territory

Abandoned and vandalised cars

Children playing in dried out river bed

Invest in gold. BENSON and HEDGES

TAKE AWAY
MEALS EATEN
TABLE
20¢ EXTRA

Territory store

Mobile school
Northern Territory

Wooden water containers and coolamons made from the knots and boles of various trees.

Desert landscape
Northern Territory

'We don't want something for nothing.
It's not good to get something for nothing.
In the old days, we did a day's work, we got a day's pay.
Some of the white guys, they were alright,
they treated you fairly, they looked after you.
They were good bosses,
but you knew you had to do a day's work.
I don't know what happens now.'

— Old woman, who used to be a
stockwoman, on the Roper River.

'Aborigines dancing at Brighton,
Tasmania (1836)' Oil painting
by John Glover.
An early European view.
Courtesy Mitchell Library,
Sydney.

Helicopter mustering in the bush

Aboriginal stockmen mustering cattle

Stockyards

The youngest stockman pulls himself up onto the rails as the bullock lunges past, blood spurting from its horn stumps. Bawling and swinging spume, it seeks another victim. The old man gives a startled yell as he's charged.
"He's all yours, son,"
"No, Boss. You take him. He too damn big for me . . ."
The others laugh.
The broad brimmed hats are discarded outside the yard, in the dust. The sacs of testicles are thrown casually through the rails, as the kites circle. Scarlet blood and wrinkled brown hands on the weathered wood. The beasts are pulled over by the truck from the lassoo, then leg-roped — it takes three men. The old man clowns as he bends over, backside in the air, with the small, sharp castrating knife in his hand. Then the boy in the red shirt brands the animal, taking the iron from the greybeard whose job it is to watch the fire.

Aboriginal stockmen in stock camp

Cattle dog at work

Aboriginal stockman

Tribal Aborigine

Northern Territory landscape

Tropical rainforest

Exploratory drilling

Full scale mining

Albert Namatjira, a full-blood member of the Aranda tribe of central Australia, was born at Hermannsburg in 1902. He was baptised with the name Albert, later adding 'Namatjira', his father's tribal name, to his signature on paintings. His education included instruction at the Hermannsburg Lutheran mission school, as well as initiation at thirteen into tribal life. At seventeen he eloped with Ilkalita, a Loritja girl, whom he was tribally forbidden to marry. For three years the couple lived and worked on surrounding cattle stations, until Namatjira received word that the marriage was accepted and he and his wife were able to return to Hermannsburg. In 1934 he was taught the technique of water-colour painting by the Australian artist Rex Battarbee, and he began to paint pictures of the landscape of central Australia. He sold his first painting for five shillings in 1936. This was the beginning of what came to be known as the Namatjira school of art. In 1939 the National Gallery bought one of his paintings, its first acquisition from an Aboriginal artist. In 1945 he built himself a two-room sandstone cottage, complete with modern amenities and a flower and vegetable garden, at Hermannsburg, where he continued to live and paint. In 1957 Namatjira was one of the first Aborigines to become an Australian citizen, a step which, among other privileges, allowed him to buy liquor. He had already, however, been allowed the privilege of paying taxes. Around this period, tribal obligations which involved him in the support of large numbers of relatives led him into debt, and he also began drinking heavily. This led him into conflict with the law. He was subsequently charged with supplying alcohol to his relatives on the reserve, and in March 1959 he was sentenced to imprisonment for some months. In August of 1959, aged fifty-seven, he died in Alice Springs Hospital, a disillusioned and somewhat bitter man regarding his people. At the time of his death he was probably the best loved and most widely known of all full blood Aborigines. The London Times devoted almost 200 words to his obituary.

Michael Leslie lives in a small modern flat in the Sydney suburb of Glebe. The plain white walls are hung with traditional bark paintings by Aboriginal artists. He earns a reasonable income supplemented by a single parent's income, as he looks after his small son from whose mother he is separated.

'My father worked on the railways and as a child we moved all over the place in N.S.W. country towns right up to Charleville in Queensland. I left school when I was seventeen, didn't get the School Certificate and came to Sydney where I got a job through Aboriginal Employment with the Public Service. I was also doing dancing part time with a dance centre on City Road. Someone told me I should go and see someone at the Aboriginal and Islander Dance Theatre but I did nothing about it until eventually one of the teachers invited me over. I hadn't previously been interested in Aboriginal culture of any sort and now I realise I missed something. I didn't meet any full blood Aboriginals until then. I don't speak an Aboriginal language but my great grandmother did. My great grandfather had French and Negro blood and jumped ship to live in Australia. Both my grandmothers were Aborigines and my father's mother told me all the family history and has many old photographs going back several generations. When asked I say I am Australian. If they keep asking I explain a bit more. If you're mixed blood white people are harder to get on with than Aborigines and won't sit next to you on buses and trains even if it's the only seat left and they stare at you if you are with a white girl. People keep saying whites treat blacks badly. That's not completely true. They don't treat them any differently than blacks treat blacks in other countries. I went to Nigeria with the Dance Theatre, and it felt good to walk among so many black people. It felt good not to be a minority. But I wouldn't like to see it in Australia. If I'm going to be black I'd rather be black here. We went to some discos in Nigeria, they were in tin shacks with lino on the floors, and you'd walk down the laneways to get to them and there would be kids and adults sleeping in the laneways. That's no good. And we saw some of the places where the rich people lived. Idi Amin, other African leaders, they've treated blacks badly. It's not just a matter of black and white.

'I was brought up a Catholic, my grandmother used to make us go to church. She used to hold prayer meetings in the house. I stopped going when I was about fourteen. I believe in God sometimes. The Aborigines talk about the Rainbow Serpent, other people talk about Jesus, Buddha, all different names. You don't know. Sometimes you believe, when you think about it.

'I keep away from politics. I'm not interested. I don't go to pubs, I don't drink, I've seen what it's done to people. I just go to discos sometimes. I spend most of my free time with my friends, people from the Dance Theatre. I don't get into trouble and most of my friends don't. I try to get as much work as I can, I've got two jobs. I'd like to become a physical education teacher or do something in theatre, but you need qualifications to do that. I'd like to get a dance scholarship and go to the U.S.A., but there's a lot of people who'd like to do that, and they can only pick a few. I don't have any definite plans."

Essie Coffey is a forty-year-old full-blood Aboriginal film maker from Brewarrina, a country town in north west N.S.W. with an 85% Aboriginal population. She has lived there most of her life and as a child remembers her family and other members of the Murrawarri tribe being rounded up by whites to take to a reserve. But her father Donald Goodgabah, an elder of the tribe, "went bush" and raised his family in old tribal ways, which Essie feels gave her a love for the land and an identity as an Aboriginal.

She believes in personal freedom but has had to battle hard to attain it. She says: "In the white man's world of the past Aborigines were the baddies and white people the goodies . . . it's changing a bit now but has a long way to go. Most Aborigines who try to pull themselves up with a white man's bootlaces get awfully frustrated — they can't get jobs and they drink away their government handouts — it's the only way they think they have to get the frustration out of their system. Most Aborigines can't get up and speak out as I do — and I want my own voice to be heard loud and clear. I believe one way to achieve this is through film, television and radio. As a woman I want to make sure I am heard as widely as possible. So far the Aboriginal voice has been a cry in the wilderness. I see my people dying in the gutter from alcohol and I am depressed and frustrated about their living conditions and because of what's happening to them. They are losing their pride."

In 1977 Phil Noyce, an Australian film director, worked in the area on "Backroads", a feature film about black-white relationships. During the filming Essie met Martha Ansara, one of the crew who had filmed and directed a number of short films about women in Australian society. Together they decided to make a documentary film on Aborigines with the aid of a grant of $16,500 from the Australian Film Corporation. Martha got together the film crew and provided the technical know-how while Essie scripted, directed and appeared in "My Survival as an Aboriginal" which won the Greater Union Award for the best documentary film of 1979. It also won the coveted Rouben Mamoulin Award.

Essie sings two of her own songs in the film and is vocalist for her band "BlackImages", with which she helps to raise money for N.S.W. charities. She also represents the Aboriginal Lands Trust, The Aboriginal Advisory Council and the Legal Service.

In Dodge City, the slang term for the Aboriginal section of Brewarrina, she looks after 18 children, eight of her own and ten adopted. She teaches Aboriginal culture and broadcasts legends from the Aboriginal Dreamtime over the local radio. During weekends she tries to encourage young Aborigines to take an interest in their tribal history and culture by taking small groups into the bush to learn to live and survive and to love the land which she believes is theirs by birthright. She does all these things on a voluntary basis.

She is not "agin the government" but feels there is plenty of room for the development of better understanding and a happier relationship between black and white throughout Australia. And she looks like developing that aim for the rest of her days.

Her tribal name is Essiena Goodgabah which means Flower of the Honey Tree . . . J.J.G.

Aboriginal & Islander Dance Group I

Tribal initiation, Northern Territory

Suburban citizens, Redfern N.S.W.

She is standing in front of the empty horizon, the prototype Aboriginal woman, the one that you see in all the paintings and photographs.

She comes forward shyly, a grown woman with the manner of a small child, and offers her hand. She looks at her hand rather than at my face; it is evident that the fate of her hand is more important than my reaction to her. So I take it carefully. And then, as I take it, there is the smile. Wide teeth, white, that make her brown eyes disappear into creases, and I find that I'm smiling too. But my smile can never be equal to that wide, joyous grin. Mine is a wan Caucasian thing, barely formed, and it doesn't have the sun and desert behind it. By it, I am made aware of the distance between us.

Her hand is dry and crinkly like soft crumpled paper, dry and dusty, and the skin fits loosely over it. There is a scent of dust mixed with the smell of stale sweat that is part of her cotton dress. The dress is not made for her square body, so to fit her waist it hangs like a tent over her hips to below her knees. Beneath it her spindley legs are planted splay-toed in the dust, poised to move away into the distance. When she moves, her body moves inside the dress, unencumbered by it, not wearing it.

And there is nothing that I have to offer her. There is nothing in my face that she should recognise or value. I don't know what to do. She has taken my hand and dropped it, we have smiled at each other, and that is all.

It is another time, further back in the past. I am flying over the same desert. All I can see, far below is a red, rocky plain tinged with purple and grey. The colours are deadened by the harsh light.

It is late afternoon, and we are coming down onto the surface at Birdsville in a plane reduced by the vastness to a minute tin insect, a buzzing, metallic dragonfly. In front of us as we land is a small collection of tin-roofed buildings, surrounded by emptiness in all directions. The pilot of the plane laconically mentions that there are four cattle stations, perhaps sixty Europeans, in the surrounding thirty-six thousand square miles. And that is all.

The American tourists, with whom I am hitching the ride, appear stunned. It all seems too improbable, this vastness and heat. The door opens and we feel the air burning as we draw it into our lungs, dehydrating our skin, drawing out the moisture.

When we leave the town, I have an image in my memory of a painted brick pub, white plaster, paint flaking away, floors dusted with powdered sand. Flyscreens of rainbow plastic strips in the doorways, a vase of plastic gladioli in the empty fireplace. Outside, the pillared verandah shades an earth floor and a sleeping dog, and offers a little relief from the interminable heat haze. Everything is powdery and dry except for the sticky flies that cluster around our eyes.

Europeans have made little impact on this landscape. Many Australians have never seen it. Many Australians are hardly aware of its other inhabitants at all.

The settlement south of Alice Springs consists of the pub, the hotel, the police station and the post office. The main street is of dirt, lined on one side by a row of fibro cottages for the men who work on the railway line. The cottages are all of a basic design, but each is painted in one of six pastel colours to vary the monotony. They appear odd, out of place, too real in the clear air. Behind the town is the area known as The Camp, a littered sprawl of humpies and shacks. Sketching an informal division, a broken-down fence of barbed wire. Then, the railway.

The Line is the *raison d'etre* of the white man's town. It is the life-line, it must constantly be repaired. The trains, 'The Ghan' (called after the old Afghan camel trains) and 'The Chaser' (because it chases the 'Ghan') sometimes take about eight hours to cover two hundred kilometres, because of the narrowness of the gauge. There are occasional derailments as sand, wind and water undermine the track. The trains bring supplies, mail, beer, and passengers to whom the Aborigines can sell hand-carved boomerangs for a dollar or two. If a plane lands at the settlement, it taxis in down the main street and parks in front of the post office.

Twelve miles further along The Line there is a gang of six 'section men' living in a cottage beside the track. They often talk to no one besides themselves for weeks on end, unless the missionary happens to go past in the truck. But they wave to the trains.

The Aborigines come into the settlement from the desert because it is the source of their monthly cheques from the government. Most of their money goes to the local store. The store is a tin shed that the health department has made motions to close down because it sells meat across a dirt floor. All purchases are entered in a notebook against the credit of each Aboriginal's social security cheque, and are accompanied by tins of soft drink from the freezer. The supply of clothes is in the charge of one of the fettler's wives (four dollars for a dress). It is a foreign enough landscape.

The American tourists, pleasant people, interested, are visibly distressed by the huge number of aluminium soft drink cans that litter the settlement for a radius of a mile.

'Why aren't they taught?' they ask.

You attempt a tentative explanation. It would seem, you say, that for thousands of years the people left behind the things they no longer needed. Their possessions were few because they were by nature nomadic. So that for thousands of years the items of wood, bone, clay, stone, bark, and skin became part of the earth again.

And then white people brought a drink with mysterious bubbles that was sweeter than . . . what? Honey ants? A drink that is vastly attractive to the black people. So they buy it. When the drink is finished, the can is dropped. And it does not become part of the earth.

You say that therefore the black man's aesthetic perceptions don't fall into a dichotomy of natural and unnatural, and that therefore the concept of litter does not exist. But it all seems a little irrelevant. What remains is that the stage for the Great Australian Tragedy, the deterioration of the tribes, is a vast plain of red earth and rock scattered all over with aluminium tubes that glitter blindingly in the sun. They even out-number the beer bottles along the railway line.

Since then, I have written to Mac, the missionary at the settlement, now and then. I've said I'd like to come back to look around, lend a hand for a little while, on the way further north. He has written back, an almost illegible scrawl on a scrap of paper: yes, come. It reaches me in Sydney in a battered manila envelope.

I arrive about seven in the evening while dinner is being served on the train.

I say goodbye to the section workers with whom I've been playing poker, and jump off the high step. The heat outside the train is intense. I carry my bag along the gravel beside the track. No one else gets off. The other passengers watch from behind the glass of the windows and doors.

Mac appears, a slight figure in shorts, thin like a grass-hopper, with a sandy beard. There is a small knot of people beside the station master's office waiting idly to see what the train has to offer. We help unload the bread from the goods van into a truck.

Mac tells me that I can sleep in the caravan, which is his residence. He will take his sleeping roll onto the back of the truck. We load the bread, and the truck takes us the half mile to the camp.

I have a shower in the tin shed behind the new store, and a black crow struts outside the window apparently watching me. Or perhaps it is the water that is attracting it.

And then as it begins to darken, I go for a walk around the town. Still there are the piles of rubbish and the shanties, the row of rusted trucks and disused machinery over which the Aboriginal kids climb like rabbits in a warren. I meet some of the people; again there are the dry, paper-skinned handshakes and the initial shyness. As I walk past the pub, a huge half-Aboriginal man bellows out from the lighted doorway: It's the sheila! Come in and have a drink!

Overhead, there is the huge starry sky, ever-present as it only can be in desert regions.

We do the rounds on the back of the truck.

Topsy — an immense old woman with the cracked, loose skin of a goanna, that hangs in folds — wants to move camp. We pick her up from under a tree a few kilometres outside the settlement.

One does not question why she is sitting there alone. She tumbles herself over the side, her breasts lolling hugely over her stomach underneath her dress. She has with her a few cloth bundles and a tarpaulin, a kerosene-tin of water and an uncovered saucepan full of cold, clotted stew. She settles herself in like a Buddha among the floppy slacks, rolling with the bumps and chewing tobacco. The boys have been loading her things slowly and carefully, one at a time, working from the outside to the middle, and now she is enthroned for the ride in state.

We unload her a mile away at a five-foot-high tin shack containing three dogs and two men, one of whom is her husband. He is wearing dark glasses. He stares, black face and black glasses peering from the dark interior, quite unmoved by the arrival of his lady. She strolls majestically towards the shack, and we disappear in a cloud of dust to perform the next small job.

On another day I collect the odd bits of clothing, sweat and dust encrusted, that are discarded around the settlement. They are in a process of gradually merging with the dirt. I put them through a washing machine in one of the sheds — the water turns red brown, so I put them through again — and hang them out. They dry immediately, stained but clean and warmed by the sun, and the one-time owners come by and take them from the wire strung behind the shed. Not so much reclaiming them, but accepting them into their possession again. It is a futile occupation, because they will be similarly discarded when they are again too dirty to be worn.

Mac walks past and watches, neither approving nor disapproving. One must do something.

I clean out the food cupboards in the store and wipe the shelves, check and sort the first aid supplies, make a rubbish dump in a corner of the allotment and collect together the debris, and stack the useable building materials. Working in the mornings and the evenings, resting in the middle of the day. Even after a few days, a sense of timelessness sets in. I might have been here for years. The smiling children cluster round the van to watch, but until they get used to me, they are petrified into silence if I look at them or speak to them. So I ignore them, until having an idea, I sit down on the floor and start to draw pictures in an exercise book. Then they creep around, curious, and at last take the pencil out of my hand.

Some days later, after the stores are done we drive down to the bed of the Finke River for a picnic with some of the women and children. There are blankets to sit on; bread, cold meat and billy tea, the last much too strong and sweet, to eat and drink.

The black kids teach me how to sit in the sand and sift through it for *yulchas* — little onion-shaped bulbs about six inches down, hard to see among the pebbles. We cook them by burying them in the hot sand under the campfire, where they pop like popcorn. The children pull them out of the raked-out coals with their bare fingers, but when I try I burn myself. They laugh.

Then we sit under the eucalyptus trees until late afternoon. There is absolutely nothing to look at, nothing to do, but drowse in the shade. After a short time, the black women sink into a trance-like state, and I follow their example.

After about five hours like this, the mind goes on strange journeys. One doesn't feel consciously bored, but when nothing happens to mark the passage of time, one becomes conscious that time has little meaning. Perhaps it is these deserts of the mind that are the breeding ground of the Dreamtime.

Later I go for a walk along the dry river bed. It is silted up with fine, soft sand, there is the occasional bleached shell of a water snail. Small yellow wildflowers grow, where there is no water for a long way below the surface. When I climb up onto the rocks, about fifteen feet up, there is a breeze that is cool by comparison with the air at ground level.

But when I look around, standing there on my rock, I can see no apparent sources of food or water at all. Except for the yulchas, which I would never have found without the aid of the children.

Mac tells me that the people, instead of hunting, sometimes go out into the desert in search of tectites. These are smooth pellets of igneous rock believed to have come from the underside of the moon. Thumbnail sized, and shaped like tiny flying saucers from whirling through space, they lie scattered in thin tracts across the desert.

We go out to find and bring back a group of tectite-hunters from about a hundred and twenty kilometres out. Mac knows approximately where they are. We pack food and water on the assumption that we could break down and be stranded for days, and we tell the policeman where we are heading. It is only a hundred and twenty kilometres, but it takes four hours in the four-wheel drive vehicle. The air inside the cabin becomes painfully hot, and after a while it is impossible to put an arm down on the burning, vibrating metal of the door.

When we arrive, through some mysterious means of navigation of Mac's, we find the usual camp. A number of old women and an old man, their dogs, and a tiny kitten wrapped in a blanket. They have a plastic bucket full of grey meat, charred on the outside, smelly, and seamed with yellow fat. The old man tells us proudly that they killed a kangaroo.

Proudly, also, they show Mac the plastic bags of tectites. The old man giggles about a freak stone which is a perfect replica of a penis, about an inch and a half long. He shows it to Mac, but with a show of embarrassment he tries to hide it from me.

Mac buys the tectites, the perfect ones individually and the damaged ones by weight. He usually sells them at a slight loss to geologists and rock shops. It provides a small income, but more than that it is something to do.

In the afternoon we bump back to the settlement across the invisible road, the whole party of tectite-gatherers in the back.

You could call it our street, I suppose. First there's the caravan, where I sleep. Next to it is parked the truck where Mac sleeps, and next to that is the packing crate where Cliff, who is building prefabricated houses, lives. It is a large crate, it has a bed in it, a tool bench, a small stove and a tape recorder. It is pretty-well furnished, all things considered, for a crate.

Late at night we sit in the light coming from the doorway of the caravan and talk, sometimes till two in the morning. Once the sun sets and it is cooler you feel revitalised, you wake up a little. The cigarettes glow in the warm, dry darkness.

Cliff is a slim, sunburnt man with an easy smile and long hair that he flicks back and holds in place with a broad-brimmed hat. With his shirt off and a cup of coffee hooked onto his finger, he squats back on his heels and tells stories with a deliberately casual air. He wanders from a description of opal mining in Coober Pedy to an account of a gun battle with a group of Yugoslav miners, and then to crocodile shooting in the Gulf. From shooting crocodiles to hunting buffaloes in Landrovers, and then to working on rich men's yachts along the coast. It appears that, having come into the settlement from somewhere else, he has taken the job of supervising the Aboriginal housing project because there was no one else around. He likes Mac, he tells us privately, but doesn't like the system he represents.

Mac gets argumentative at times. He is a thin, energetic man who could be any age and who is starting to show the effects of living in isolation. Set in his ideas, a little eccentric. We've heard stories that he's been in trouble for treating the people too roughly when they're drunk. But he explains himself: he gets tired of having the women arrive repeatedly at the caravan in the mornings with their heads split open, so he occasionally knocks down one or two of the men so that they know how it feels. He thinks the Department hasn't removed him firstly because there is no one to replace him, and secondly because the people like him. The last statement is true.

The job itself is a little harder to describe. It includes, for instance, 'shifting the woodies'. The woodies are the prefabricated wooden huts supplied by the government for temporary housing. But according to tribal law, when someone dies, the people must move camp. This used to be a very practical idea where disease was concerned, but now it merely means that the woodies are left empty while the people move into the bush. So Mac puts the woodies on the back of the truck, one by one, and moves them to the new camping ground . . .

Not all the stories are humorous, he continues.

A while ago a baby girl crawled onto sacred ground, where no women were allowed, while its mother was not watching. Both the baby and the mother were executed by the tribe. The police don't interfere with tribal matters in case of causing an apparently endless chain of retribution. For whom do you arrest? All the tribal elders? Or the man delegated to do the spearing?

And take a man who does not really understand the theory of possession, he adds. Things are owned communally by the tribe, one uses what one needs if it is available. Black takes a shovel he sees lying on the ground and uses it to break firewood. Then he leaves it where he used it.

The shovel is the same shovel, it has not altered its state. But White calls him a thief because the shovel has been stolen from him. Black is possibly a little puzzled that White feels about a shovel the way that he feels about a wife. Game and check.

So the uneasy co-existence goes on. The government supplies housing but makes little allowance for teaching a nomadic people how to live in it. Then the dirt, the fires on the floor, the broken windows reinforce the criticism against the people.

The young men want to go to Alice Springs, where there are movies, bright lights, excitement. And then, not finding the mysterious fulfilment that these things promise, they roam the streets in drunken gangs, quick to turn violent . . .

There is no sound in the camp except the occasional barking of a dog. Perhaps that's why we talk. To ward off the vast silence and the ghosts. At any rate, the conversation at night becomes a regular thing. There is a sense of being stripped down to essentials, and behind the essentials, something not understood.

They tell me in the pub that Mac sleeps with the black women. On the evidence that the black men say so. They laugh. He's a randy bastard, they say, I should look out that he doesn't have a go at me. They also say that he cheats the people in the store when they're too drunk to know the difference.

They're arrogant, tanned young men and they seem to balance lightly on the balls of their feet, waiting for something to happen. They wear riding boots, which denotes they work on the land, and open necked shirts. Their eyes are a cold blue and narrowed prematurely by the sun. They offer to take me to the Alice in their plane in return for a night out on the town. It's almost a challenge.

They talk about the young black women, the girls, who hang around the pub and put the hard word on the men at two dollars a time. But they're contemptuous. When a gin looks good you've been too long in the Territory, they say. They call the men who associate with the black women Gin Jockies. All the same, there are a lot of half-white babies around the settlement.

Mac has told us that the Aborigines themselves think he sleeps with the black women. He explains the rumour like this. When he takes the young girls back to the camp after ticking them off for hanging around the pub, sometimes they throw a drunken clinch on him. The men see the tracks in the morning, the interlocking footprints and the scuffle, and there is no way his denial will be believed. So it goes.

In the pub, the web of gossip among the white men becomes more and more intricate, more and more damaging. I hear stories of men murdered for sleeping with other men's wives, of suicides and madness. It seems that the climate of the place is such that small dramas can easily become big ones, random accusations produce psychological growths that feed like mushrooms on the tedium and the isolation. Someone points out the black tracker, a good looking but disdainful Aboriginal in the corner, who wears khaki and a hat with a police badge. Evidently a few weeks ago a white man went berserk and ran off into the desert. The tracker found him a day and a half later, in a crouched position, dead and dehydrated. He died scrabbling for water in the dry sand. Another man who became accidently lost was not so lucky: he wasn't found for two weeks, and Mac had to gather his remains in a sack 'after the dingoes had been at him'. Sometimes, it seems, there is no way out.

The day passes, long stretches of heat interspersed with welcome darkness. The end of the month comes.

As dusk sets in on the evening of the day the Government cheques are given out, an old man and his wife wander over to a shallow depression in the ground, seemingly randomly chosen, and squat down. Then another drifts in and joins them, and another. Soon there is a small ring of people. Around the ring circle the flagons of sweet, red wine.

Later, intermittent wails and screams sound through the night as the old men take out their surly drunkenness on their wives, and vice versa. Little Allie shambles past the caravan, holding his baggy pants up, followed blindly by his old lady. He tries to hit her, loses them, and falls over. Henry James and Teddy Boy (who gives them these names?) have a fight, staggering over sheets of tin and breaking bottles. The noise is appalling. Cliff yells out from the crate: there's a bloody woman trying to sleep in that bloody caravan, and all hope of sleep vanishes. But Henry James and Teddy Boy have already stumbled off into the darkness.

These are the tribal elders.

So next morning the police truck is in action. It is a four-wheel-drive with an iron cage of two-by-four netting on the back. Teddy Boy is sitting in the cage, looking dejected, rocking slightly.

The jail is a small tin shed about twelve feet by twelve feet, hot and airless, isolated. But it is not the jail that the old men mind. It is the humiliation of being seen driven through the camp, caged like an animal.

Cliff, in sympathy, sometimes hides the old men under an empty water tank when the local cop is out looking for them. As he says, there's not much point in the whole exercise. It will be the same again next time. And the time after that.

A day later the news comes through that a woman has died in the camp. Cliff and another man go down to lay her out, and the people start to dig a grave. Mac reports the death to Alice Springs. The visiting nurse states that it was caused by a heart attack, although this is complicated by a head injury she received in a fight.

Then, for some reason, the message passes around that the coroner at Alice wants the body for an autopsy. Mac has to explain this fact to the people, but it is inexplicable, seen merely as another example of the white man's strange ways. Mac becomes worried. The people believe that the spirit won't rest unless the body is buried in traditional grounds. She won't have the dignified burial they would have given her. He thinks there may be trouble.

But the body must be got underway quickly, because of the heat. There is no refrigerated cask, not even a plastic bag. So Cliff sets out in his car, the body on the back seat, knowing that it will start to decompose before he arrives.

The incident sets a certain indefineable mood on the camp. People walk around restlessly, saddened at the death, but restless also.

The visiting nurse tells me about her child care groups. She has learnt the local language, but there the difficulty only begins. She tells me, for instance, that the culture of this particular tribe does not include the concepts of choice, of asking questions, and of making decisions in the present that will affect the future. It occurs to me only then that I have never heard one of the older people ask a question. When in the store, they tend to stare blankly until Mac says: you will need some meat, some soup. And so on. But all the same, I find myself staring at the woman in disbelief. She explains that to find something out, she tells a story, and the Aboriginal women tell a parallel story in return. It is difficult to grasp the difficulties in communication that these facts represent. I tell her so and she laughs. Where I would be paralysed into a kind of existential hopelessness, she goes ahead and acts.

The time comes to leave.

On the last morning I watch Nora washing the black babies, assembly belt fashion, under the shower. Nora is one of the older girls. Mac brought her back from Alice Springs where, he said, she was taking on up to a dozen men a night for a couple of dollars. Now she is sixteen, a tall friendly kid who laughs continually. The sores from the venereal disease are all gone. But it is hard to tell what she really thinks.

The babies stagger around covered with soap and grinning from ear to ear, almost overbalanced by their pot bellies. There is a progression through from dark brown to light brown to light pink without any firm divisions. Once the soap is washed off they dry in the sun in a few minutes and wander away like chickens let out of a coop.

It's a quiet day, still very hot. I sit in the shade and a lame crow limps past. It's a particular crow that I know by now; it hangs round the camp a lot, made distinctive by its drunken, rolling hops.

I am waiting for the 'Ghan' to come down the track in the mid-afternoon. I know I'll be able to hear it for quite a while before it arrives.

It's hard to leave. I haven't been here for long enough to be part of the place, but it's still hard to leave.

The Cattle Stations

The late afternoon sunlight streams down on the ridges, illuminating the low scrub and the bright yellow of the winter wildflowers. Over the homestead and the camp, clouds of kites wheel silently and slowly in the clear air. Towards evening we go out with Tommy in the truck, carrying the camp gear and the saddles, the enamel wash basins and the iron pots and the tin boxes with the supplies. These contain a bag of flour, a couple of pounds of sugar, some packets of tea, tins of golden syrup, meat, bread for the first day. One of the younger Aborigines takes the horses, stringing them out in a long line, leaving early enough to have them ten kilometres out by sundown. I pack my duffle bag with a sleeping bag, an extra blanket, a change of clothes and a toothbrush. The other black stockmen throw their swags on the back of the truck, throwing themselves on after them, and we take off.

We leave the homestead behind, with its interior of soft beds and comfort, hot water and meals on tables and conversation, and head into the openness of the gibbers and gathering evening.

Tommy, the camp cook, stretches a rope between two trees and drapes the fly over it, pulling the canvas taut and straight and pegging it with iron stakes. The canvas forms an open-sided shelter about seven by seven metres. He sets up a wooden table in front of it and starts dragging in fallen trees for the cook fire. We manoeuvre for places, casually throwing down our swags where we'll be most sheltered and yet nearest the warmth of the fire. Further away the black stockmen set up their own identical camp, with their own camp cook. Further away still, the jingle of the now-hobbled horses.

Then the helicopter arrives. Having flown the two hundred kilometres or so from Alice Springs, it lands a short way outside the camp, and the blades jerk to a stop. The pilot jumps out and walks towards us, a bright patch of blue denim against the dull, grey-green scrub. He is a young, bearded man who wears Mexican silver rings and a chain round his neck, and, compared to us, he is also quite clean. I brush some of the rust from the cooking irons and carbon from the charred logs off on my jeans and walk up to shake hands. They call him Piccolo Pete, or, on occasion, the Agitated Ant.

He, also, unloads a swag from the helicopter and throws it under the fly.

At night the sky is so clear that the stars shine through the navy-blue blackness like points of ice. We roast one side of ourselves against the burning embers, turning from one side to the other as we sit on our swags, on kerosene tins, on stumps of wood. Roy, the owner's son, borrows a Phantom comic from one of the young black stockmen, along with a tin of Log Cabin tobacco, and some cigarette papers and sits reading it by the light of a kerosene lamp. We eat beef with thick slices of buttered bread to sop up the meat juices, and drink tea that has brewed itself so black in the billy ʾhat the concentrated tannin is almost enough to make you gag. The Aboriginal stockmen huddle close to their own fire. Each camp is a little island of light and warmth in the surrounding cold.

In the morning Tommy rolls out of his swag with a grunt at six and gets the cookfire burning from a tree trunk still alight from the night before. Breakfast is tea and damper. We wash in an inch or two of cold water in the enamel basin. Further over, the other camp is also stirring.

I walk over to where the hobbled horses are grazing and one of the black stockmen, the old one, helps me catch my horse. Previously, he has shown me how to fit the hobbles — I've never used them before, don't know how tight or loose to buckle them, or whether above or below the fetlock. The man, with his seamed face below a battered and dirty felt hat, nothing like the crisp Akubras the younger men sport, never looks at me. He does not address me. If I ask him a question he answers monosyllabically, his eyes elsewhere. He ignores my thanks. But there is no hostility. He is too old for it to be likely he is under a tribal taboo against speaking to women, I think it is just that as I do not really fit into the scheme of things, am out of place in the men's camp, so he prefers to ignore my presence as much as possible.

He is half a head shorter than me, with bandy legs in old grey trousers. He wears an ancient leather coat softened and moulded with time to fit his barrel body. He seems immeasurably old. His jowls disappear into the creases of his neck, his wrinkled throat disappears into a creased and stained, but clean, cotton shirt. He treats the horse expertly but disinterestedly, slipping on the bridle with practiced movements, but not deigning to pat it. He hands the reins to me silently and I walk back from the stockmen's camp towards our own.

In the meantime the pilot has walked out to the helicopter, a piece of smooth and perfect technology out of place in the dry grass and the early morning sunlight, and started his pre-flight drill. In a little while the *ker-chug* of the rotating blades invades a silence so far broken only by the sounds of men's voices, the odd clatter from the camps, the neigh of a horse. The Aborigines always watch the movements of the helicopter with some attention, although they never go near it, or exhibit any curiosity about how it works. It is nothing to do with them, it is enough that it is there.

Then the stockmen ride up from their camp, we split into two parties and move off. Roy and I and the old man angle away into the scrub at a fast walk, while the younger Aborigines take another direction. We wind in single file through the trees, dodging and ducking under low branches. The vegetation here is so thick that the horses have to break a path through with their shoulders, shying and picking up their hooves as the low thorn bushes prick their legs. Shrubs pluck at our thighs and tangle with the stirrups, catch at our reins. Somewhere in the midst of all this, I have been told, there are cattle. We ride in silence for about a mile. Then suddenly the old black stockman takes off on his horse at a gallop.

In half a second Roy has taken off after him, and after a moment's hesitation I take off, also at a gallop, after them both. I have heard and seen nothing, but I follow in their general direction, keeping my head down in the horse's mane to avoid the branches. Then all at once bellowing cattle are racing in all directions, yelling stockmen on horses are breaking out of the scrub after them, and I still do not know where I am supposed to be going. I follow the greatest amount of noise and finally crash into a clearing along with the mob. It appears that by pure luck I have turned up at the right place at the right time.

For some hours we drive the mob parallel to the main ridge until we reach the track branching off to the artesian bore and the cattle yards. Then, at 10.30 in the morning, we take time off in relays for lunch. Tommy, along with the Aboriginal camp cook, has mixed up a damper and cooked it in the camp oven, packed up the camp, and shifted to the turn-off to meet us. He provides tea and steak, then moves on to the next night's campsite to set up the camp anew. We, in the meantime, continue herding the cattle along the track. I fill a position as an outrider and take my distance and pace from the black stockman nearest me, a boy in a red shirt and a wide-brimmed hat. We have the mob yarded by six in the evening.

Tommy is waiting in the new camp with the billy boiling, and when I slide off my horse and hit the ground for the second time in ten hours my legs buckle under me. The Aborigine's indefatigable.

In the camp that night the men tell yarns. Tommy has concocted a mustard yellow beef curry, which we eat with bread and white rice. I crawl into my sleeping bag on the hard ground, insulated from some of the cold by a length of canvas, and as the cattle bellow and mill in the yards a couple of hundred yards away, fall instantly asleep.

Again, the Aboriginal stockmen keep close to their own campfire. At night the spirits are out, one does not move around.

It is said that when cattle were first introduced to the grasslands of the Northern Territory, the Aborigines were so puzzled by the strange creatures that they thought they might be human, and tried to talk to them. That was at the end of the last century, when the tribesmen still had the interior of Australia largely to themselves. Then the cattlemen moved in and took possession of the land, not quite so long ago as most people think.

The Aborigines adapted quickly, learnt to ride horses and learnt the psychology of the cattle in the same way they had learnt the ways of the animals they hunted. Then they worked as stockmen.

In the past, mustering was done entirely on horseback, with the black stockmen and the station owner often away from the homestead for months at a time. Often, it was only the black stockmen who could find the cattle at all, as they ranged between water sources scattered over thousands of square kilometres of territory. Then light planes came to be used for reconnaissance, and the job became simplified. With the advent of the helicopter, the job could be cut down to a matter of weeks.

To muster by helicopter a number of riders are sent out whose function it is to gather together a nucleus mob and hold it together. The helicopter works from the outskirts to the centre of the area being mustered, making low sweeps and stampeding the beasts in the right direction, tilting the stragglers in towards the main herd. As the cattle come in, the riders on the ground take over. When the nucleus mob is large enough, it starts to move. The principle is quite neat, quite simple, quite elegant; but in practice it involves wild cattle, heavy scrub, treacherous scrub bulls and, for the riders, no over-view of the whole operation. Here the horsemanship and the knowledge of the country of the Aborigines is essential. The cattle stations could not function without them.

On the cattle stations, Aborigines tend to live in groups and clans roughly in the territory they regard as their own. In many cases, they do not see why they cannot co-exist with the whites who also occupy it, although in some cases this reasonable approach has hardly been reciprocated. The camps are situated near, but not too near, the homestead, because this is usually the location of the school, the store, and often the water supply. Quite often the station owner has an honorary position in the tribe, if the association has been a long one. He may be asked to help solve problems, mediate with outsiders, and usually co-operates in providing medical care. In return, the group provides stockmen and household help. Obviously this system has been fraught with problems aggravated by racism, abuse of the Aborigines' rights, alcohol, and wage inequality, but in some cases it can work. From observation, this is one of the places where mutual respect is sufficient to make it work.

At lunch time next day, I watch the old man drinking his tea. The camp fire flames flicker almost invisibly in the bright sunlight, only the shivering shadow of the smoke on the red dirt evidence that it is alight at all. There is a slight breeze. He forks the black tin out of its nest of ashes with a stick, taps the side once or twice to settle the suspended leaves. No move he makes is hurried.

There is little about him in the clearing. No shade. The trees are not designed for shade, their thin leaves hang vertically down and the shadows they cast are sparse. The shifting air is drying, rather than cooling. He squats down on his haunches among the red ants that scramble on the sandy soil, oblivious to the heat, he is comfortable in that position almost indefinitely. He drinks the tea scalding hot, a dark ochre red, with lots of sugar. Tea is a habit adopted enthusiastically from the white man. His horse is tied to a tree some little distance away.

This man has worked as a stockman, on and off, for maybe thirty years. He is also a fully-initiated Aboriginal, a keeper of the law. He and the other elders conduct the initiations and perform circumcisions. He has a position of respect in his community. On this station he is also spoken of with respect by the white men he works with, although on many he wouldn't be. He trusts the white man as far as he has to, does not accept a new idea until he has examined it and is convinced of its rightness. He keeps his own thoughts behind a barrier of reserve and politeness, a thorough training received as a keeper of sacred ritual and ceremony. He is not impressed by people who talk too much. A white man is part of the environment, not his tribe, he will use his finely developed instincts to take advantage of him for his own survival, if he can. But where he has accepted him on trust, he will fulfil obligations as he would to a member of his tribe. He is honest, although his unwillingness to display his thoughts is sometimes taken as dishonesty. Essentially, he is independent.

He squats in the dust, apparently half-asleep, but there is very little going on in the camp of which he is not aware.

Concerning him also, there is an incident on the muster that I particularly remember.

Occasionally one of the half-grown bull calves with budding horns, called Mickies, would break away from the others and have to be wheeled back in. Sometimes they'd put their heads down and run, refusing to change direction and head back to the mob. Once or twice I chased these Mickies until I lost them in the scrub a half mile away from the main herd. The second time this happened the Mickey propped suddenly, turned, and charged my horse, catching her full in the lower shoulder. The horse staggered, grunted, and stopped, but didn't go down. The bull turned and trotted away into the trees.

After I'd made sure no injury was done to the horse, I rode back to the mob, feeling angry and useless at losing the bull. It wasn't until this second failure that I noticed the old stockman on his white horse quietly appearing out of the scrub a few minutes after me. No one made any comment. He had been, in the words of the boss's son, keeping an eye on me. I hadn't even known he was there.

It is a short muster, this time. After three or four days we go back to the homestead. Life at the station continues as it did before we left it. Later will come the branding and the trucking; heavy and exhaustive work involving the building of temporary yards, the roping and wrestling of each calf to the ground to be branded and marked, the drafting and loading of bullocks onto road trains.

Meanwhile the black children play in a wilderness of abandoned vehicles not far from the camp. The Aborigines tend to spend their money on second-hand cars, abandoning them when and where they break down. It is easier to go walkabout in a car than on foot. The older girls still go out with the women, hunting goannas, gathering witchetty grubs and honey ants. They show us these last: insects with outsize amber beads of sweet syrup attached to their tiny, shiny black bodies, kept fresh in a billy under green leaves. They refer to this as 'bush tucker' and regard it as a favour to be given a lift in the truck to the specific place they want to go to find it. The families spend a lot of time in the creek bed, away from their huts, washing, cooking, or just sitting. I go for a walk along the white sands of the creek, occasionally seeing children peering from tree trunks or over sand banks, curious to see what I am doing. Sometimes they track me, following invisibly until their laughter gives them away. Then they become quite cheeky, calling out names that I, perhaps fortunately, don't understand. If I come across one of the older women, she will return my greeting, but is shy of attempts at conversation from a stranger.

I have had it made clear to me at the homestead that one respects the privacy of the camp. Even the owner does not go there unless invited, for a specific reason. The last time the owner's wife was there was to assist at a difficult child birth. So I steer clear of the tin shanties and huts, and the pre-fabricated schoolhouse which is not now in use.

But half a mile along the creek bank I am halted by something unusual. Laid out in the smooth white sand there are miniature cattle stations, looking exactly as they would if seen from the air. There are roads of carefully graded sand, river fords of pebbles, uniform fences of fine twigs stretching for dozens of metres, cattle yards and out-buildings. There are roofless homesteads with many rooms, complete with internal doors and windows, trees and gardens, lawn and outhouses, water tanks and fuel dumps and machine sheds. There is also a camp. The buildings are built of cardboard, about four inches high, other things are constructed of wood and plastic, bottle caps and other paraphenalia from the rubbish dump. But everything, the fences and the trees, is in proportion. There are three boys about twelve years old playing in one of these cattle kingdoms, and they seem highly embarrassed at my intrusion. They stop pushing the off-cuts of wood that represent vehicles over the network of roads and fix their eyes on the ground. And although they eventually overcome their shyness and talk to me, I soon leave.

What impresses me is their ability to gather information and fit together a model of something they can never have seen as a whole. To me, the powers of observation demonstrated by the children are formidable. But at this stage I am no longer surprised.

Moving on, further north, nearer the sea, the situation changes. Here, on the boundaries of Arnhem land, relationships between black and white are sometimes violent.

Sometimes the local blacks get drunk and come into the scattered homesteads from the settlements with shovel-nosed spears, looking for trouble. The cattlemen's conversation is studded with accounts of past confrontations. The station managers and owners are tough, often uneducated, often autocratic and uncompromising. Isolation makes them rigid in their ideas; they feel they are fighting for what they've got.

A policeman passing through has shown me a confiscated shovel-nosed spear. The shaft is an inch thick and stands taller than a man. The head is a ten-inch iron blade, sharpened on both sides and coming to a shovel-shaped point, hence its name. It is not a throwing spear, it is for stabbing.

The policeman considers that the northern Aborigines are of more mixed blood — Chinese, Islander, European — and this makes them a little more crazy than the purer tribes of the interior. Such assumptions are widespread.

Here, on this station, I sleep on an iron bedstead under a tin-roofed verandah, a brown dog under my bed.

We eat workman-size meals at a big communal table; after dinner we sit in the concrete-floored living room, telling the inevitable yarns. The boss loves to talk. A big, erratic man of uncertain temper, all his reactions are physical, exaggerated. He lounges back in a chair with a bullock-hide over it, boots left outside the door to the verandah, feet outstretched in grey socks. The boss doesn't drink, but anyone else is welcome to a can of beer or the traditional heavy slug of Bundaberg rum. On the walls there are buffalo horns a metre and a half across. The other decorations are paintings on black velvet and Marlboro posters. The two women of the household talk about shooting dogs, I listen to threads of various conversations under the repetitious, nasal whine of Slim Dusty on the battered record player.

The boss talks about the Aborigines a lot. But he doesn't call them Aborigines. He calls them 'niggers' and 'coons' and 'boongs'. He is open in his dislike, reverting almost obsessively to the subject.

'Tell you a funny story,' he says.

'Seems that when the local cop goes into town, he takes his dog on the back of the truck. Doesn't want him running round the place while he's in the shops, so he puts him in the cells. On his way out he runs into one of these Legal Aid blokes nosing round. So he says to him, "Look mate, there's a character in cell No. 6 I reckon you better have a word with. One of your mob."

'So the L.A. bloke goes in and has a look around and comes back with a funny look in his eye. "I don't reckon", he says, "that that's very funny".

'Cop looks him straight in the face. "He's black and he's a mongrel, isn't he?" he says. "I reckon that makes him one of yours." '

The stories are all in a similar vein. The men sit up yarning and drinking till after midnight.

We go out after buffalo in some of the most desolate country I've ever seen: trees blackened from some long-ago fire, charcoal-grey dirt and dirty blond grass, crumbling slate. A few lean bullocks toss their horns and canter away from the Landrover, sending up puffs of dust through the ash. The Toyota negotiates eroded gulleys and knocks down dehydrated saplings and crumbling scrub, and we chase a buffalo, a rangy old man, which makes rapidly-decreasing runs before baling up in the river. Every stop the boss's sons climb out with the gun, and the explosions from the 303 seem to reverberate for miles, but the scrub is too thick to get a clear shot. Eventually we lose the beast in the gathering darkness with a flesh wound in the shoulder. There are no lights on the Landrover and we have to be back at the homestead before night. On the way home we pass odd groups of Aborigines heading towards the town in old Holden cars, but they stare at us suspiciously. There is little friendly feeling between the Aboriginal settlement up the road and the local whites. The boss is angry at the boys for missing the buffalo. So tonight the atmosphere is tense.

Tonight, also, a black from another place, a man called Snow, a relative of one of the local people, has arrived in the station camp. He has a chip on his shoulder against the boss, he has said he wants to 'fix the white bastards'. One of the local men comes up to the homestead and tells the boss there might be trouble. On behalf of the camp, he wants the man to be told to leave.

'He no good, that feller,' he says.

But the boss says:

'He's one of your mob. You tell him to leave.'

One has the impression the boss does not go out of his way to avoid trouble.

Later, Snow walks up to the homestead and appears at the kitchen door, swaying. In the background, some of the other men have gathered in little knots.

The boss walks up and stands in front of him, forcing a confrontation.

Snow looks at him.

'You white bastard', he says.

He takes a swing, but he's drunk.

The boss ducks back lazily and hits him on the jaw. The black man goes down, but then he gets up again, touching his mouth and looking at his fingers. Then he calls out to the others.

'Come and help me, you mob. Look, I got blood comin' out of me mouth. You seen what he done to me.'

But the other men don't move. They won't necessarily side with an outsider; they have already made their judgement of who is right and who is wrong, and it is against Snow. The boss turns his back on the scene and walks back into the house.

Later still that night one of Snow's children, whom he has brought with him, falls out of a tree and splits open the side of his face. Snow brings him to the school teacher, the school teacher brings him to the house. We hear the child moaning as we finish eating dinner. Duncan, one of the older men, is holding him down with gentle hands, as Duncan's daughter dribbles disinfectant over the gaping wound with cotton wool. He must be hurt badly, because Aboriginal children rarely cry. With each moan, the old man's forehead wrinkles.

The boss says:

'You want to kill me, do you? Yet you bring your kid here when he falls out of a tree.'

Snow says nothing.

The school teacher takes the child to the hospital on a nearby settlement in one of the trucks.

Later, Duncan and Doreen come to tell the boss that they've moved Snow off the camp, sent him on his way.

'We don't want any trouble', they say. They are prepared to be fair, they want to be allowed to live in peace. They know that if there is trouble, they will be the ones to lose out in the end.

A day later I sit in the fine dust under one of the widespreading trees with the school teacher and Doreen. Doreen is Duncan's wife. Duncan is one of the leaders, one of the oldest men in the camp. Doreen has snow white hair and a kind, wise face, she wears a clean cotton dress and bare feet. She used to be a stockwoman when she was younger.

She tells us she thinks that the 'blackfeller and the whitefeller should work together'. And that you should work for money, not hope to get something for nothing. Or does she? Maybe she's just telling us what she's learnt that white people want to hear. It's hard to tell.

We are stripping the black outer leaves from scarlet, bulb-like grass roots, to make dye to dye the pandanus to make baskets. If the women and girls start to make baskets again, with the encouragement of the school teacher, they can be sold in shops in Katharine. Which will mean a little independence, a little pride, for the local people. To peel a bag full of roots takes most of the afternoon, but it is peaceful to sit in the shade with this quiet woman.

But in the evening the boss looks at me curiously.

'So you're a nigger-lover, are you?' he says. 'You ought to hang around a bit. You might learn something.'

It seems the station owners up here can't make money. Some of them have walked off their properties with no more than when their grandfathers walked on. Three generations, in some of the most promising and yet the most heart-breaking country in the world, wet following dry, watching the cattle dying of diseases and transport prices spiralling until they lose money just by doing a muster. So it's good to have a scapegoat, something concrete to blame. The Aborigines get everything for nothing, he feels, he has to pay taxes to support them. The boss drifts onto one of his favourite subjects: one of the many government schemes to aid the Aborigines to become self-sufficient. He sees it as a waste of money and land that he and others like him could use to better effect.

'They give this mob of niggers up here a couple of hundred thousand dollars to start a cattle place', he says. 'They're going to run it themselves, they think. Well, first thing they do is they buy up a whole lot of cars and trucks and drive them around all over the place to see their friends and relatives. Don't put any oil in them, so they stop. That's the end of the cars. Then they get themselves all togged up. I tell you what, R.M. Williams in Brisbane must've made a fortune out of them. They buy all their stockmen all sorts of gear – ten gallon hats and lairy shirts. *And* they're paying them $250 a week when there's no muster on. This goes on for a while and then the government blokes realise they're not doing all that much about the cattle side of it, so they give them another couple of hundred thousand dollars. So they buy 3,000 head of Brahmin Cross and let them loose. Of course, the cattle go bush. I reckon they think they're going to build a fence around them after they let them go. I tell you what, they're improving the bloody scrub cattle though. So the government gives them some more money and they buy 140 head of broken horses from Queensland. Comes the wet season they let them go, too. Don't see them again, either.'

'Then they reckon they'll start a pub up there. Get in about a hundred and thirty kegs and really lay into it. There're fights and killings and they're all staggering round the place laying into each other like you wouldn't believe. So the coppers fly in a DC3 full of police and they get out and lay into them, and there's a bloody riot. Then five or six blokes on the place who don't drink take the cops to the kegs and they start splitting them open with axes. So there's beer everywhere and coons with plastic buckets and plastic bags carting it away over their shoulders. Takes the cops three days to get 'em sober enough to cart 'em off and charge them.

'You don't read about that in the papers down South. They wouldn't be game to print it . . .'

There is very little I can think of to say. It is the failures that are most immediate, rather than the over-all plan, here where the tensions are most apparent.

We leave the homestead and camp one night on the Roper River, on the road to a deserted homestead on an abandoned property. The eucalypts on the river bank are afloat with butterflies, there are white spoonbills and pink water lilies on the lagoons. Beyond the sucking mud there are little running fish that skip over the surface of the water and rest camouflaged among the fallen leaves on the periphery. All in a narrow area of extraordinary beauty between the river and the desolate plain. Beyond this again is the plateau of Arnhem Land, with its weird rock formations and strange and fertile lands, its mangrove swamps and its tribal mystery.

I wash my clothes and hair in the river, knee deep in mud, and then sleep through the hot afternoon in the elusive shade of the trees. There is a full moon in the evening, a bright night glittering with stars. I sleep on the ground outside my tent, under the huge vault of the sky, woken intermittently by plops and rustling noises in the water and river vegetation. There is plenty of time to think about theories of historical necessity, of the natural recession of anachronistic cultures, of all the easy words that account for nothing in the destruction of a people. My dreams are inhabited by gigantic crocodiles and rainbow snakes that shift lethargically in the bowels of the earth. Perhaps they are dying, as the systems of belief that have kept them alive for so many thousands of years are dying. There are only a few Aborigines left capable of renewing the culture. Soon it will be too late.

The City and The Tribe

Above the desk in the front office of the Aboriginal Legal Service in Redfern there is a not-very-expertly executed picture of a court room, painted by a convicted murderer. The most striking feature about it is that all the members of the court are black, except for the man in the dock, who is white. After an initial moment of shock, this can, of course, be easily dismissed as propaganda of the crudest kind. What one is forced to consider is why the initial moment of shock occurs.

Before the arrival of Europeans in Australia two hundred years ago, most Aborigines lived as semi-nomadic hunters and gatherers along the fertile coastal plains and rivers, with only small numbers in the desert zones, although these included areas as arid as the Nullabor Plain. The largest social grouping was the tribe, which rarely, if ever, operated as an entity. The tribe was further subdivided into clans, although the basic economic unit was the family: a man, his wives and children. The system was communistic, and roles were fairly strictly defined. The men were the hunters of large animals, the fishermen; the women and children were the gatherers of plants, smaller animal life and insects. In pursuit of food, groups moved from area to area within their own territory, either seasonally or to allow an area to regenerate itself. Almost everything in the environment that was edible formed a part of the food supply, although this in turn was regulated and protected by tradition and taboo. A hunter might not be allowed to kill the totemic animal of his clan, for example, or a certain part of that animal might be reserved for the tribal elders, thus ensuring that they were guaranteed a food supply when too old to hunt. Conservation measures such as selective killing, and regeneration measures such as burning off, were not unknown. It would also appear that, prior to European occupation, the Aborigines only found it necessary to exploit a small part of the resources available to them, and that local Aboriginal populations only expanded in proportion to the ability of the environment to support them in the leanest of times. As a result, a certain amount of leisure time was available for cultural pursuits, and it would be a mistake to assume that the system of nomadic hunting and gathering as it was practised constituted a miserable, hand-to-mouth existence.

It is estimated that there were some five hundred and seventy-four tribes in Australia, speaking as many as two hundred and sixty separate but inter-related languages (apart from local dialects). The reason for this fragmentation of language was that different groups of Aborigines tended to live and roam only within their own traditional territories. The languages themselves were of considerable grammatical subtlety, with a system of prefixes and suffixes to modify the meaning of a root word which often ran into thousands of variations. Vocabularies were particularly well-developed in relation to ritual and to the physical environment. In a form of cultural exchange, songs and myths were passed from group to group through corroboree or by travelling composers, new songs and stories were considered 'dreamed' or 'found' rather than created.

According to the Aboriginal concept of the world, there was a period before man inhabited the earth when ancestral spirits in human and animal form wandered freely, and, in the course of passing through the country, shaped the physical environment. Rivers and water holes, hills and rock formations were all created in this way, and the locations of particular epic struggles between the spirits became sacred sites. The descendants of these spirits became real men, animals and birds, and the spirits also passed on the laws and customs according to which the creatures of the world were to live. To remain in harmony with the life forces of the universe as they knew it, it was necessary for the Aborigines to live in a close relationship with the physical environment. This connection with the spirit realm, or Dreamtime, was maintained through ritual and ceremony, and celebrated and passed on from generation to generation in song, chant, dance and artistic expression, in which all members of the clan participated.

Membership of clans, with their individual animal, plant or insect totems, was either patrilineal or matrilineal, according to region. Marriage between clan members was forbidden, but members were permitted to marry those with a certain corresponding relationship within another clan. This helped to avoid too close inter-breeding within groups. Two of the most significant events in tribal life were the initiation of male children and the occurrence of a death. The former was conducted in stages, beginning with circumcision and progressing through various stages of secret education in law, myth and magic. The women of the tribe conducted a similar secret life, and although it is generally considered not to have been as complex as that of the men, there were powers and rituals exclusive to women. When a death occurred it was considered necessary that the spirit of the dead person be aided in arriving safely at its spiritual home, so that the process of incarnation and reincarnation could continue. Otherwise that spirit would be left to wander in the void between life and death, possibly making trouble for the living. All deaths except those of the very young and the very old were believed to have been caused by sorcery, and in the process of finding and punishing the person responsible, sequences of revenge and counter-revenge were often started between groups, although these matters could often be settled by peaceable means.

Material possessions were few, simple, versatile and easily replaceable. They included weapons and implements, often with a dual function. The weapons and utensils that were kept for any length of time were often finely decorated, both to record the myths of the artist's clan and to imbue them with special powers, even to make them acceptable to the totem of the animal they were to kill. And while it has been argued that the Aborigines were technologically unsophisticated, an ability to exist unencumbered by material goods could be regarded as admirable by a society unconditioned by consumerism. It can also be argued that the Aborigines developed to a high level of performance powers which in Europeans are either atrophied or, at best, in a primitive state. The former include an exceptional self-discipline in the face of pain, and also the senses of hearing, sight and smell, as demonstrated by their almost uncanny ability to track animals and 'read' the environment to predict weather changes, food availability, animal behaviour and the activities of other Aborigines in the area. The latter includes the use of telepathy over long distances, auto suggestion (in sorcery), foreknowledge of future events and other aspects of parapsychology, the existence of which are undisputed in Aboriginal culture.

From a population of some three hundred thousand at the time of the arrival of Europeans, numbers of Aborigines sank to a low of sixty thousand by 1921, and have only recently begun to rise. In the late 1970s there were estimated to be about forty-five thousand pure blood Aborigines, and about one hundred and six thousand of mixed descent. The decrease was due to a combination of factors.

Following European settlement, thousands of Aborigines died of previously unknown diseases such as smallpox, venereal disease, tuberculosis, whooping cough, measles, leprosy and influenza, to which they had no resistance.

At the same time, the introduction of sheep and cattle caused a corresponding reduction in the numbers of grass-eating mammals whose pastures they usurped, on which the tribespeople were dependant for food.

The Aborigines were also at the mercy of what have been described as 'gun-bearing rejects from British society'. Retaliatory action against Aborigines for cattle spearing or for violent resistance to having their land possessed usually far outweighed the original crime, and often took the form of wholesale massacres.* The last recorded instances of these massacres occurred in the 1930s. In other instances, usually glossed over in social studies texts, arsenic-laced sugar and flour or disease-infected clothing was deliberately distributed to fringe-dwelling groups in the form of gifts.

Later, the remnants of Aboriginal society were removed to reserves, where they were further harassed by well-meaning missionaries and laid low by the ravages of alcohol, prostitution and unhealthy diet.

During the first hundred years of settlement, official and private attitudes of the Europeans to Aborigines varied from mild paternalism to a view that they should be exterminated as a natural pest. Up until the 1930s, Government policy was based on the assumption that the race would die out naturally; from the 1930s to the 50s that the remainder could be 'assimilated' into white society and thus disappear; and only from the 1960s was a right to a racial identity recognised.

The Aborigines in turn, having retreated from the presence of the white man until there was nowhere left to go, developed the phenomenon Professor Elkin describes as 'intelligent parasitism': a system of adaptation to European settlement which allowed them to dwell on the fringes of it. This was based on the necessity for survival as the former way of life became more difficult, rather than on an inherent desire or respect for civilisation as the European defined it. But as the old life broke down, so did the fabric of cultural and religious patterns which gave the Aborigines a belief in the future and a will to survive. The cultural links with the environment were broken and the European way of life, with its Protestant work ethic and capitalist backbone, offered no satisfactory alternative to a people unable to adapt to it completely. Thus, in a time of cultural conflict and dispossession, the Aborigines as a people had no spiritual retreat, a state which has been compared, in terms of Christian mythology, to losing one's soul.

Now, in the late 1970s, most Australian Aborigines are living on the outskirts of small country urban centres and cattle stations. However, at opposite ends of the spectrum of Aboriginal existence, there are two vastly different polarities. For the purposes of description, one can be designated Urban, the other Out-station.

In Sydney alone there are fourteen thousand five hundred Aborigines living in the city area, mostly in the inner-city suburb of Redfern. Although almost without exception they are of mixed blood, and usually two or three generations away from tribal living, they identify themselves completely as Aborigines.

Many come from a generation of families which have, until recently, been split by a Welfare Department able to make arbitrary decisions as to whether a child is neglected, and having done so, to put that child in a home. Many have been victims of an education system little able to cope with the cultural differences that being Aboriginal implies. Few have skills or educational qualifications that make them readily employable. Many have, from a young age, been alienated from white society by repeated arrests and imprisonments for drunkenness, vagrancy and petty crime.

These Aborigines, who drift to the cities in search of work, tend to be young. There is little future for them around the small country towns from whence they come, just as there is not much future for the young whites. They find accommodation with friends or family members who have already made the move, congregating in ghetto-like conditions. They

*In the case of the Tasmanian Aborigines, descended from Australian Aborigines who crossed to Tasmania some 12,000 years ago, the entire race was wiped out in what is arguably the only successful act of genocide committed by a nation

are not popular with white landlords, who know that a house or flat let to a black family may eventually become a communal centre for a large number of people, with the problems that such over-crowding entails.

Then there is job prejudice, in a city already burdened with unemployment. The percentage figure for Aborigines unemployed is estimated to be six times higher than that for the community at large. Some of these Aborigines will never be employed.

Then there are problems of health. Until recently, many urban Aboriginal children were suffering from undernourishment to the point of permanent brain damage. Many country children still are. This is not due to a lack of food so much as a lack of knowledge about nutrition: an addiction to sugar and carbohydrates to the exclusion of fresh fruit and vegetables. Many adult Aborigines are alcoholics. Recent research has indicated that inherent metabolic differences in Aborigines as a race, particularly in relation to the body's ability to process sugar and alcohol, are partly responsible for this poor standard of health. In a country with one of the highest standards of living in the world, the average Aboriginal still dies twenty years younger than the average white.

And yet, in spite of this unpromising situation, or perhaps because of it, a new consciousness is arising. Aboriginal voices are making themselves heard. Aboriginal members of the community are taking a hand in their own destiny through participation in organisations concerned with Aboriginal health, housing, social security, legal rights, land rights, local administration, education and culture. The Aboriginal section of the urban population is becoming a political force, along with other minority ethnic groups. It is producing leaders. As a direct result, there is a growing interest by white Australians in Aboriginal culture and the place of Aborigines in contemporary society, to the extent that in 1976 the Australian National University commenced offering a set of inter-disciplinary courses in Aboriginal studies. Aborigines themselves are achieving higher levels of education and expressing a desire to use it to help their own people. And their future appears vastly more optimistic than it did ten years ago, when an interlocking attitude of self-defeat appeared to be the norm.

At the other end of the scale is the phenomenon sometimes known as the Outstation movement.

From the mid 1950s onwards, an increasing number of Aborigines began to manifest a desire to move away from European society and live in their own communities, closely associated with those areas to which they felt a traditional religious and cultural tie. Combined with a long history of labour exploitation and wage inequality, of diversion of government funds and wages by unscrupulous property owners, of discriminatory laws and outright racism, was the knowledge that they, unlike the American Indians, never ceded their land by treaty, or yet were driven off it in a state of war. The land rights movement came into being, as far as white Australians were concerned, with the now famous incident in 1966 when two hundred stockmen of the Gurindji tribe at Wave Hill cattle station in the Northern Territory went on strike for better pay and conditions, the first such act by Aborigines in Australia's history. When the stockmen and their families moved to an area within the boundaries of Wave Hill station sacred to their tribe, and set up a permanent camp, it became apparent that they wanted more than improved living quarters. Although their petition to the Governor General, eight months later, seeking the return of some thirteen thousand square kilometres of land was refused, the land rights movement became a *cause célèbre*.

After a long struggle on the part of Aborigines and other sympathetic groups, Australian Government legislation came into force in 1977 to enable Aborigines to regain ownership of traditional tribal lands in the Northern Territory, then under Common-wealth jurisdiction. The Aboriginal Land Rights Act gave Aborigines ownership of about 20% of the Northern Territory, land which was formerly reserves. It provided legal machinery to acquire more. It also expressed a recognition of the validity of Aboriginal traditional law and cultural values.

The Australian government at that date expressed the hope that the State governments would use the legislation as a model and follow suit in their own territory. However, the States have shown a marked reluctance to do this where it would appear to conflict with the interests of mining and tourism. The legislation directs that permission for mining and other activities can only be granted by the Aborigines — with the proviso that a decision regarded as being against the national interest can be over-ridden by the Australian Parliament. Minerals on territory owned or leased by Aborigines remain the property of the government, although mining royalties are payable to the Aboriginal groups concerned. The communities, and the land on which they are based, are administered by local Aboriginal Councils, and their advisers, which liaise with the Government bodies whose responsibility they are.

Whether these communities can achieve their aims, to live self-sufficiently and in accordance with traditional values, in the face of conflicting interests remains to be seen. However, they are succeeding in creating an environment where Aboriginal languages, art, myth and law can be revived and passed on to future generations of Aborigines. If for no other reason than that the Australian Aborigines are a unique race of people, this must be seen by all Australians as a worthwhile aim.